THE One & Only salads Cookbook

NEW HOLLAND

THE
One & Only
salads
Cookbook

All the recipes you will ever need

With a Foreword by
Jenny Linford

NEW
HOLLAND

First published by New Holland Publishers in 2012
London • Cape Town • Sydney • Auckland

www.newhollandpubishers.com

86 Edgware Road, London W2 2EA, United Kingdom

Wembley Square, Solan Road, Gardens, Cape Town 8001, South Africa

1/66 Gibbes Street, Chatswood, NSW 2067, Australia
www.newholland.com.au

218 Lake Road, Northcote, Auckland 0746, New Zealand

Created by
Pulp Media, Richmond, London

Project Editors: Emma Wildsmith and Helena Caldon
Art Director: Susi Martin
Illustrations: Tracy Turnbull

Photography: Charlotte Tolhurst, Stockfood Ltd, Philip Wilkins: 60-61, 84-85, 128-129, 172-173, 194-195, Shutterstock.com: 1, 2, 6, 10,14, 17, 18, 223, 224-5, 233, 238-239.
Every effort has been made to credit photographers and copyright-holders. If any have been overlooked we will be pleased to make the necessary corrections in subsequent editions.

Publisher: James Tavendale
www.pulp.me.uk

A record of this book is available from the National Library.
ISBN 9781742572444
Printed in China
10 9 8 7 6 5 4 3 2 1

"To make a good salad is to be
a brilliant diplomat — the problem is
entirely the same in both cases.
To know exactly how much oil
one must put with one's vinegar."

Oscar Wilde

Contents

Foreword

By Jenny Linford

Salads offer the creative cook lots of scope. While for many a simple assortment of green leaves remains the iconic salad, the reality is far more varied and interesting. Salads come in numerous forms: savoury, sweet, hot, warm or cold. They range from hearty concoctions, based on pasta, potatoes or pulses, to light, elegant, leaf-based creations, favoured by those watching their waistlines. Salads can be created using meat, fish and seafood, vegetables, fruit, grains and pulses.

The secret to great dressings

A good dressing has a wonderfully transformative effect on even the simplest salad, lifting it from the dull to the enjoyable. It acts as a pick-me-up, giving zest and zing to ingredients from earthy lentils to noodles.

A classic French-style vinaigrette consists of olive oil to wine vinegar used in a ratio of three to five parts oil to one part vinegar. Place the wine vinegar in a bowl, season with salt and pepper, whisking until the salt has dissolved, then add in the olive oil and whisk until well-combined. Alternatively, place all the ingredients in a clean-lidded jar and shake until thoroughly mixed.

Olive oil, with its distinctive, sophisticated flavour, is a classic choice for making salad dressings. Do, however, try experimenting with other oils, such as walnut oil or hazelnut oil, with their distinctive toasted nutty flavour, to achieve different results. Similarly, vary the acidic element of the dressing by substituting lemon juice, lime juice, grapefruit juice, orange juice or verjus for the vinegar. Vinegars, too, offer scope for variation. A dressing made with a good quality, mellow balsamic vinegar will taste very different from one made with a more restrained Spanish sherry vinegar or delicate rice vinegar. The vinaigrette can be further tweaked by adding in flavourings such as a touch of mustard, a little sugar or honey, crushed garlic or chopped fresh herbs.

When making your salad dressing, match it to the contents of your salad. Delicate fresh salad leaves require a lightly-flavoured dressing, while more robustly flavourful ingredients can take a bigger hitting dressing, flavoured say with crushed garlic and balsamic vinegar.

One simple but golden rule to bear in mind with many salads, especially leaf-based ones, is to dress them at the last minute, that is **just before serving**, in order to prevent them becoming limp and sodden.

Making Mayonnaise

Another traditional salad dressing is mayonnaise, which adds a luxurious creaminess to salads such as potato or coleslaw. Although it has an intimidating reputation, in fact, making your own mayonnaise is very simple, although patience is required.

It's very important to have all the ingredients, including the eggs, at **room temperature**. Use 1 egg yolk for 150ml oil. Light-flavoured oils such as sunflower are recommended for mayonnaise rather than strongly-flavoured olive oil, although a combination of sunflower and olive oil works well.

Whisk the egg yolk with a pinch of salt, add in 1 tsp of vinegar or lemon juice and whisk again. Now gradually add in your oil, at first just a drop at a time, whisking thoroughly all the time. As the mixture begins to emulsify and thicken you can add the oil in a thin, steady trickle, still whisking continuously. The finished mayonnaise should have a thick,

but smooth texture. Once made, the mayonnaise can be flavoured to taste, for example, with crushed garlic, ground saffron soaked in a little water or chopped fresh herbs.

Putting together your salad

When creating a salad, do bear in mind you want combinations that work either by harmonising or contrasting nicely. While variety has a part to play, using too many disparate ingredients can simply result in a salad that lacks clarity and impact.

Using good-quality ingredients is key, especially for raw salads. Look for the freshest and tastiest, seasonal vegetables, fruits and herbs that you can find, so, for example, ripe, sweet tomatoes rather than dull, insipid ones.

Make sure your salad leaves are thoroughly dried before you toss them with the dressing. Salad spinners are an effective way of drying them; alternately place them between layers of kitchen paper.

Vary the textures within your salad. Combine crisp, firm-textured ingredients such as red pepper or cucumber, croutons, fried or lightly toasted nuts with soft ingredients such as lettuce leaves, tomatoes or avocado chunks.

Use colourful ingredients to make your salad visually appealing. Sprinkling in sprigs of fresh herbs, edible flowers such as nasturtiums or chive flowers or chopped fruit are all simple ways of adding vibrancy.

Warm Jerusalem artichoke and mackerel salad

1. Cook the artichokes until easily pierced with the tip of a knife; this should take around 15 minutes. When they are cooked, drain and cut into quarters.

2. Place the artichokes in a large salad bowl along with the flatleaf parsley.

3. Whisk together the dressing ingredients and pour over the artichokes. Toss the artichokes to coat with the dressing.

4. Flake over the mackerel fillets and serve.

Preparation time: 5 min
Cooking time: 15 min
Serves 4

650g peeled Jerusalem artichokes
small bunch of flatleaf parsley,
*   roughly chopped*
4 smoked mackerel fillets

For the dressing:
1 shallot, finely chopped
1 tbsp chopped tarragon
80ml rapeseed oil
40ml sherry vinegar
2 tbsp mayonnaise

Beetroot carpaccio salad with smoked salmon and baby capers

1. Cook 2 of the beetroots in boiling salted water until cooked through and easily pierced with the tip of a knife, this should take around 30 to 40 minutes. When cooked, chop into quarters. Whilst the beetroot is cooking, peel the other beetroots and thinly slice using a mandolin.

2. Layer the raw sliced beetroots over 2 plates to fill the surface area of both.

3. Whisk together the dressing ingredients and toss the cooked quartered beetroots in half of the dressing and arrange over your 2 plates.

4. Sprinkle each plate with capers and the purple radish sprouts. Divide the salmon between the 2 plates, draping the slices over the beetroot.

5. Finish by drizzling over the remaining dressing.

Preparation time: 5 min
Cooking time: 40 min
Serves 2

4 small beetroots
10g alfalfa sprouts
2 tsp baby capers
100g smoked salmon

For the dressing:
40ml extra virgin olive oil
20ml red wine vinegar
1 tbsp honey
½ grated red onion
2 drops of Valencian orange extract

Broad bean, pea and smoked trout salad

1. Cook the broad beans and peas in a pan of boiling water for 5 minutes before draining and removing the skin from the broad beans. Place the podded broad beans and peas in a large salad bowl along with the dill, pea shoots and shaved courgettes.

2. Whisk together the dressing ingredients and pour over the salad, tossing to combine.

3. Flake in the smoked trout and serve.

Preparation time: 10 min
Cooking time: 5 min
Serves 4

400g broad beans
200g peas or petit pois
1 small bunch of dill,
    roughly chopped
20g pea shoots
4 baby courgettes, shaved
    into ribbons
250g smoked trout fillets

For the dressing:
60ml extra virgin olive oil
2 tsp Dijon mustard
juice of 1 lemon
¼ tsp sugar

Baby courgette, fennel and chorizo salad

Preparation time: 5 min
Cooking time: 5 min
Serves 4

2 bulb of fennel
12 baby courgettes
olive oil
150g chorizo
4 tsp fennel seeds

For the dressing:
60ml extra virgin olive oil
30ml balsamic vinegar

1. Slice the fennel into ½cm thick diagonal slices, then slice the courgettes into 3 diagonally. Toss the vegetables in a little olive oil.

2. Add the chorizo to a hot griddle pan and cook for 1–2 minutes, allowing the oils to be released. Add in the fennel seeds and the vegetables and griddle until dark lines appear, then flip over and repeat on the other side.

3. Whisk together the dressing ingredients and toss over the vegetable mixture.

4. Serve immediately.

Crab and avocado salad

1. Lay the salad leaves out on a large plate. Peel and chop the avocadoes and scatter on top of the leaves.

2. Whisk together all the dressing ingredients and season to taste.

3. Drizzle the dressing over the leaves, making sure they all get an even coating of the dressing. Finish by scattering over the picked crab.

Preparation time: 5 min
Serves 4

70g mixed leafs such as baby gem, rocket, green oak leaf
2 ripe avocado
300g picked white crabmeat

For the dressing:
2 tbsp crème fraiche
40ml lime juice
80ml rapeseed oil
2 heaped tsp Dijon mustard

Coleslaw

1. Mix the cabbage with the carrots.

2. Mix together the mayonnaise, vinegar and soured cream. Season to taste with salt and pepper.

3. Stir into the cabbage and carrots. Cover and chill overnight.

Preparation time: 10 min
    plus 12 h chilling
Serves 4

*300g white cabbage leaves,
    finely sliced
150g carrots, cut into strips
70ml mayonnaise
1 tbsp white wine vinegar
100ml soured cream
salt and pepper to taste*

Beef and vegetable salad with peanuts

1. Preheat the oven to 400°F (200°C). Heat the oil in a roasting tin and brown the meat on all sides. Cook for 20 minutes. Remove from the oven, wrap in foil and leave to rest in the turned-off oven.

2. Blanch the carrots, beans and broccoli in a pan of boiling salted water for 5 minutes. Drain and rinse in cold water and drain again.

3. For the dressing: whisk together all the ingredients and season to taste. Mix the blanched vegetables and spring onions with half of the dressing.

4. Slice the beef thinly across the grain and mix lightly with the dressing and vegetables. Arrange on a large plate, drizzle with the remaining dressing and scatter with peanuts and chilli.

Preparation time: 25 min
Cooking time: 25 min
Serves 4

1 tbsp oil
500g piece beef sirloin
250g carrots, cut into matchsticks
250g green beans
200g broccoli florets
2 spring onions, sliced

For the dressing:
6 tbsp lemon juice
6 tbsp sunflower oil
1 tsp sesame oil
1 tsp sugar
1 tsp ginger, finely chopped
1 garlic clove, finely chopped
100g roasted peanuts, to serve
1 green chilli, very thinly sliced, to serve

Rice salad with green asparagus, peppers and sweetcorn

Preparation time: 5 min
Cooking time: 6 min
Serves 4

12 green asparagus spears
1 green pepper, diced
1 red pepper, diced
juice of 1 lemon
6 tbsp olive oil
salt and pepper, to taste
400g cooked long grain rice
2 tomatoes, diced
½ bunch spring onions, sliced
150g canned sweetcorn
basil leaves and lemon wedges,
  to serve

1. Cook the asparagus in boiling salted water for 6 minutes. Add the peppers for the last 3 minutes. Drain and rinse in cold water. Drain again.

2. Whisk together the lemon juice and olive oil. Season to taste with salt and pepper.

3. Stir into the rice, then stir in all the vegetables.

4. Divide the salad among the serving plates and garnish with basil and lemon wedges.

Rice noodle salad with ground meat and nuts

1. Cook the rice noodles in boiling, salted water for 4 minutes. Drain and rinse in cold water and leave to drain.

2. Heat the oil in a wok or frying pan and brown the meat. Add the shallots and the garlic and cook for a few minutes, then season with salt and pepper. Remove from the wok and set aside.

3. Whisk the egg and fry in the hot wok. Chop and set aside.

4. For the dressing: whisk together all the ingredients.

5. Toss the noodles, meat, egg and vegetables with the dressing. Divide the salad between 4 plates, scatter with coriander and cashew nuts and serve with a wedge of lime.

Preparation time: 15 min
Cooking time: 10 min
Serves 4

250g thin rice noodles
1 tbsp oil
300g minced beef
2 shallots, finely chopped
3 garlic clove, finely chopped
salt and pepper, to taste
1 egg
3–4 leaves Chinese cabbage, shredded
1 tomato, chopped
1 red pepper, chopped

For the dressing:
2 tbsp peanut oil
2 tbsp fish sauce
1 tbsp lime juice
2 tbsp vinegar
½ tsp sambal oelek
½ tbsp sugar

To garnish:
½ bunch coriander, shredded
40g chopped cashew nuts
1 lime, cut into wedges

Asparagus and orange salad

1. Heat the olive oil and quickly cook the asparagus and shallot. Deglaze with Noilly Prat and orange juice.

2. Stir in the sugar, salt and pepper to taste and bring to the boil. Simmer gently to reduce slightly. Leave to cool.

3. Arrange the chicory leaves and orange segments on serving plates with the asparagus and olives and sprinkle with pine nuts.

Preparation time: 10 min
Cooking time: 10 min
Serves 4

4 tbsp olive oil
400g asparagus spears
1 shallot, chopped
40ml Noilly Prat
2 tbsp orange juice
pinch sugar
salt and pepper, to taste
chicory, leaves, torn
2 large oranges, peeled and
*   segmented*
70g black olives, pitted
2 tbsp chopped pine nuts, toasted,
*   to serve*

Grilled tuna steaks with kidney beans and tomato salad

1. Drain the kidney beans and rinse under running water.

2. Mix together the beans, red onion, peppers, tomatoes, 1 tablespoon olive oil and lime juice in a bowl and set aside.

3. Mix the garlic with the remaining olive oil and add the lime zest. Season with salt and pepper.

4. Brush the fish with the lime oil and grill for about 3 minutes each side or according to taste.

5. Mix the parsley and mint into the bean salad and season to taste.

6. Arrange the tuna and salad on plates. Garnish with the mint leaves and lime wedges.

Preparation time: 5 min
Cooking time: 25 min
Serves 4

200g canned red kidney beans
1 red onion, finely chopped
1 green pepper, finely chopped
1 red pepper, finely chopped
3 tomatoes, deseeded and finely
    chopped
3 tbsp olive oil
salt and pepper, to taste
juice and zest of 1 lime
1 garlic clove, finely chopped
4 tuna steaks
1 tbsp finely chopped parsley
1 tbsp finely chopped mint
mint leaves and 4 lime wedges,
    to serve

Rocket salad with citrus fruits

1. Peel the citrus fruits with a sharp knife, removing all the white pith. Separate the segments by cutting down inside the segment skin and catching any juice into a bowl.

2. Squeeze the fruit scraps by hand. Mix the juices with the honey, olive oil and salt and pepper to taste.

3. Mix together the fruit segments and rocket.

4. Arrange on serving plates and drizzle with the vinaigrette. Sprinkle with sesame seeds.

Preparation time: 5 min
Cooking time: 10 min
Serves 4

1 orange
1 pink grapefruit
1 lemon
1 tbsp honey
1 tbsp olive oil
salt and pepper, to taste
200g rocket
1 tbsp sesame seeds

Aubergine and tomato salad with minted yoghurt dressing

1. Heat 2 tablespoons oil in a frying pan and fry the aubergine slices on both sides until golden. Drain on kitchen towel.

2. Slice 2 tomatoes and dice the remaining 2.

3. Mix the chopped tomatoes with a sprinkling of salt and pepper, the remaining oil and the garlic.

4. Mix together the yoghurt, a little salt and pepper and the mint.

5. Place a tomato slice on a slice of aubergine. Place a teaspoon of the yoghurt mixture on top and finish with a slice of aubergine. Repeat with the remaining slices.

6. Arrange on a serving plate and spoon the chopped tomatoes in the centre. Drizzle with the remaining dressing. Scatter over the mint to garnish.

Preparation time: 15 min
Cooking time: 5 min
Serves 4

3 tbsp olive oil
2 aubergines, sliced
4 large tomatoes
salt and pepper, to taste
1 garlic clove, finely chopped
150ml plain yoghurt
2 tbsp chopped mint
mint leaves, to serve

Spinach chicken salad with sesame

Preparation time: 10 min
plus 20 min marinating
Cooking time: 5 min
Serves 4

4 chicken breasts, cut into bite
size pieces
2 tbsp light soy sauce
4 tbsp sesame oil
2 tbsp rice wine vinegar
salt and pepper to taste
2 tbsp sunflower oil
1 red pepper, deseeded and
finely sliced
400g baby spinach, washed
100g cooked ham, shredded
2 nori leaves, shredded
2 tbsp sesame seeds

1. Mix the chicken pieces with the soy sauce and allow to marinate for 20 minutes.

2. Mix the sesame oil and rice wine vinegar, season with salt and pepper and set aside.

3. Heat the sunflower oil in a wok or frying pan and stir-fry the chicken for 3 minutes or until lightly browned.

4. Mix the spinach with the pepper and toss in the dressing. Add more seasoning if desired.

5. Carefully toss the chicken with the spinach. Arrange the salad on plates.

6. Garnish with the ham and seaweed strips, sprinkle with the sesame seeds and serve immediately.

Beetroot salad with onions and goats' cheese

1. Preheat the oven to 350°F (180°C).

2. Brush the beetroot and onions with the oil. Sprinkle with the crushed peppercorns, coriander and mustard seeds and season to taste with salt and pepper.

3. Put into a roasting bag and add the stock. Cook for 1 hour, until tender. Remove from the bag and leave to cool.

4. Place on serving plates and scatter with the shaved cheese. Garnish with beetroot leaves.

Preparation time: 20 min
Cooking time: 1 h
Serves 4

1kg small young beetroot
3 red onions, quartered
3 tbsp olive oil
1 tsp peppercorns, crushed
1 tsp coriander seeds, crushed
salt and pepper, to taste
2 tsp mustard seeds, crushed
50ml vegetable stock
1 mature goats' cheese, shaved
beetroot leaves, to serve

Tuna with sesame crust on glass noodle and sugarsnap pea salad

1. Marinate the tuna in the soy sauce for 30 minutes.

2. For the dressing: whisk together all the ingredients.

3. For the salad: put the glass noodles into a bowl, pour boiling water over and stand for 5 minutes. Drain and rinse in cold water. Drain well.

4. Blanch the peas in boiling salted water for 4 minutes. Drain and rinse in cold water and drain again.

5. Toss the noodles and salad vegetables in the dressing.

6. Heat the sesame oil in a wok or frying pan and sear the tuna quickly on both sides. Roll in the sesame seeds and slice thickly.

7. Divide the salad between serving plates. Add a few slices of tuna and garnish with coriander.

Preparation time: 15 min
plus 30 min marinating
Cooking time: 10 min
Serves 4

800g tuna fillet
3 tbsp soy sauce

For the dressing:
3 tbsp sesame oil
1 tbsp fish sauce
3 tbsp soy sauce
pinch sugar
juice of 2 limes

For the salad:
150g glass noodles
400g sugarsnap peas, halved
4 red chillies, finely sliced
1 bunch spring onions, sliced
1 tbsp sesame oil
2 tbsp white sesame seeds
2 tbsp black sesame seeds

To garnish:
1 bunch coriander, chopped

Fruit salad brulée with grated lemon peel

1. Preheat the oven to 350°F (180°C). Butter a baking dish.

2. Put the fruit into the baking dish and sprinkle with lemon juice.

3. Beat the egg yolks with the sugar, vanilla, lemon zest and liqueur until smooth.

4. Whisk the egg white until stiff and gently fold into the egg yolk mixture until combined.

5. Pour on top of the fruit and bake for 15–20 minutes until the topping has set. Serve warm or cold decorated with lemon zest.

Preparation time: 20 min
Cooking time: 20 min
Serves 4

*1kg fruit, e. g. raspberries, apricots,
  blueberries*
1 tbsp lemon juice
2 eggs, separated
3 tbsp sugar
1 tsp vanilla extract
1 tsp grated lemon zest
2 tbsp orange liqueur
finely grated lemon zest, to serve

Smoked salmon salad

Preparation time: 15 min
Serves 4

1 tbsp white wine vinegar
1 tbsp sunflower oil
pinch sugar
salt and pepper, to taste
1 onion, sliced
1 small head iceberg
   lettuce leaves
50g cress or watercress
1 lime, sliced
100g capers
400g smoked salmon, thinly sliced
parsley, to serve

1. Whisk together the vinegar, oil and sugar and season to taste with salt and pepper.

2. Toss the onion, lettuce and watercress in the dressing.

3. Arrange on 4 serving plates and put a slice of lime on each plate. Scatter with the capers.

4. Place the smoked salmon on top of the salad and season with pepper. Garnish with parsley.

Winter salad with quails' eggs and croutons

1. For the croutons: heat the oil in a frying pan and fry the bread cubes until crisp and golden. Drain on kitchen paper.

2. For the dressing: whisk together the olive oil, vinegar and mustard.

3. Simmer the quail's eggs in boiling water for 2 ½ minutes. Rinse in cold water to cool.

4. Toss the bacon and salad leaves with a little dressing. Peel the eggs.

5. Divide the bacon and leaves between serving plates. Top with the croutons and eggs. Drizzle with the remaining dressing.

Preparation time: 10 min
Cooking time: 10 min
Serves 4

For the croutons:
3 tbsp olive oil
½ ciabatta loaf, cubed

For the dressing:
6 tbsp olive oil
2 tbsp white wine vinegar
2 tsp wholegrain mustard

For the salad:
12 quails' eggs
12 rashers cooked bacon,
*   cut into pieces*
4 handfuls mixed salad leaves

Radicchio salad with Gorgonzola, grapes and croutons

1. Mix the salad leaves and red onion in a bowl.

2. Mix together the oil, vinegar and mustard and season to taste with salt and pepper.

3. Add to the salad leaves and onion and toss to combine.

4. Put onto serving plates and crumble over the cheese.

5. Halve some of the grapes and leave some whole. Scatter over the salad.

6. For the croutons: heat the oil in a frying pan and fry the bread cubes until crisp and golden. Drain on kitchen paper. Scatter over the salad.

Preparation time: 15 min
Cooking time: 5 min
Serves 4

1 head radicchio, leaves torn
handful of lamb's lettuce leaves
1 red onion, finely diced
4 tbsp extra virgin olive oil
1 tbsp red wine vinegar
1 tsp Dijon mustard
salt and pepper, to taste
250g Gorgonzola cheese
225g green grapes, peeled

For the croutons:
3 tbsp olive oil
½ ciabatta herb loaf, cubed

Preparing asparagus

Asparagus are utterly delicious when steamed or lightly cooked and added to salads. They need only a little preparation to get the best flavour and texture.

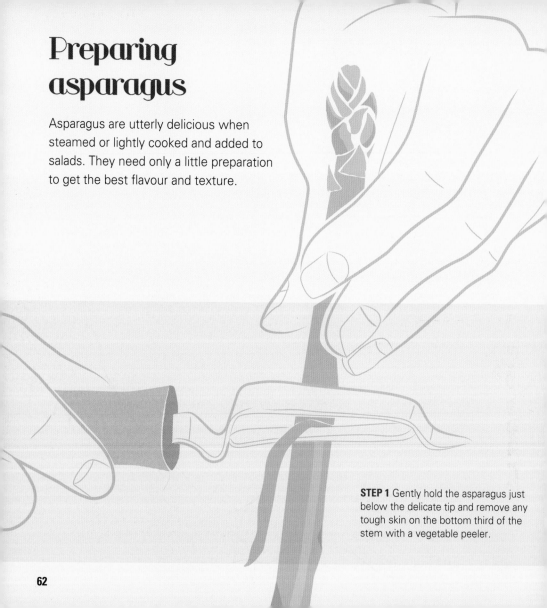

STEP 1 Gently hold the asparagus just below the delicate tip and remove any tough skin on the bottom third of the stem with a vegetable peeler.

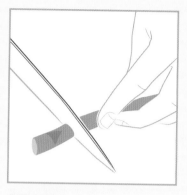

STEP 2 With a sharp knife, cut away the hard ends, or hold the stems in two hands and bend until it snaps.

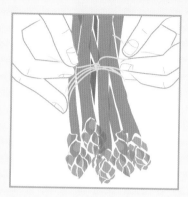

STEP 3 For ease of cooking, tie together the asparagus stems with a little kitchen string to make a bundle.

STEP 4 Put the stems into a large pan of boiling water. Cook for 3–5 minutes or until tender when pierced with a knife.

STEP 5 With a slotted spoon, remove the asparagus and transfer to a plate lined with kitchen paper and pat dry.

Salad with blue cheese, bacon-wrapped plums and apricots

1. Cook the bacon in a dry frying pan until cooked but not crisp.

2. Thread a prune and apricot onto 12 wooden skewers. Wrap 2 slices of bacon around each skewer.

3. For the dressing: whisk all the ingredients together until thickened.

4. Toss with the salad leaves and arrange on serving plates. Place the skewers and cheese on top.

Preparation time: 15 min
Cooking time: 5 min
Serves 4

24 slices bacon
12 ready to eat prunes
12 ready to eat dried apricots
200g mixed salad leaves
200g blue cheese, cubed

For the dressing:
1 shallot, finely chopped
1 tbsp white wine vinegar
1 tsp apricot jam
1 tsp grainy mustard

Rice salad with smoked trout and sesame

1. Put the rice and salt into a pan and cover with water. Bring to a boil and cook for 10 minutes.

2. Add the asparagus and cook for a further 3–4 minutes, until the rice is completely cooked and the asparagus is slightly crunchy. Drain, rinse in cold water and drain again.

3. Stir the oil, lemon zest and juice, mint and sesame seeds into the rice and asparagus. Season well with salt and pepper and leave to cool.

4. Spoon the rice mixture into serving bowls and top with the smoked trout.

Preparation time: 15 min
Cooking time: 15 min
Serves 4

250g long grain rice
1 tsp salt
250g asparagus, cut in bite-size
    pieces
3 tbsp olive oil
1 lemon, finely grated zest and juice
4 tbsp chopped mint
2 tbsp white sesame seeds
2 tbsp black sesame seeds
salt and pepper, to taste
4 smoked trout fillets, cut
    into pieces

Noodle salad with vegetables and chicken

1. Put the chicken breast fillets into a shallow dish. Mix 2 tablespoons teriyaki sauce with 2 tablespoons oil and brush the chicken with the mixture. Cover and leave to marinate for 1 hour.

2. Cook the noodles in boiling, salted water for 5 minutes, then drain thoroughly and rinse in cold water. Drain and set aside.

3. Heat the remaining oil in a frying pan and toast the sesame seeds, then stir in the curry paste, vinegar and the remaining teriyaki sauce.

4. Put the noodles, onion, carrot and cucumber into a bowl, add the sauce and mix well.

5. Heat a frying pan and cook the chicken for about 10 minutes, turning once, until cooked through. Slice the chicken breasts at an angle.

6. Mix the salad leaves and bean sprouts into the noodle salad and serve in glasses, topped with slices of chicken breast.

Preparation time: 15 min
  plus 1 h marinating
Cooking time: 15 min
Serves 4

3 chicken breast fillets
3 tbsp teriyaki sauce
3 tbsp oil
100g thin rice noodles
2 tbsp sesame seeds
1 tsp red curry paste
1 tbsp rice vinegar
½ red onion, thinly sliced
1 carrot, cut into sticks
1/3 cucumber, cut into thin sticks
50g mixed leaves, spinach, rocket
  and watercress
100g bean sprouts

Green salad of kiwi fruits, cucumber and avocados

Preparation time: 15 min
Serves 4

2 ripe avocados
4 ripe kiwi fruit
1 cucumber, cut into sticks
1 lime, juice
parsley and cucumber slices,
*   to serve*

1. Slice the avocados and remove the stones.

2. Slice the kiwi fruit.

3. Mix these with the cucumber and toss in the lime juice and some black pepper to taste.

4. Put into serving bowls and garnish with parsley and cucumber slices.

Savoury orange salad with onions and olives

1. Stir together the lemon juice and olive oil.

2. Peel the oranges and remove all the white pith. Slice the flesh, catching the juice in a bowl.

3. Add the juice to the olive oil mixture and season to taste with salt and pepper.

4. Stir the onion, oranges and olives into the marinade and leave to stand for 20 minutes before serving, garnished with mint.

Preparation time: 15 min
plus 20 min resting
Serves 4

3 tbsp lemon juice
4 tbsp olive oil
4 oranges
salt and pepper, to taste
1 large red onion, sliced
125g black olives, pitted
chopped mint leaves, to serve

Salad leaves with pears, walnuts and Gorgonzola

1. Place the salad leaves, chives and pear slices on serving plates.

2. Scatter over the walnuts and cheese.

3. Whisk together the vinegar, walnut and sunflower oils and honey. Season to taste with salt.

4. Drizzle the dressing over the salad.

Preparation time: 15 min
Serves 4

200g baby spinach leaves
100g rocket leaves
½ radicchio, leaves
½ bunch chives
2 pears, cored and sliced
50g chopped walnuts
100g Gorgonzola, crumbled
3 tbsp cider vinegar
1 tbsp walnut oil
2 tbsp sunflower oil
1 tbsp honey

Aubergine and bean salad with capers

1. Mix together the anchovies, capers, onion, vinegar, 3 tablespoons oil and horseradish and season to taste with salt and pepper.

2. Heat the remaining oil in a frying pan and cook the aubergine and peppers for 4 minutes.

3. Cook the beans in salted boiling water for 10 minutes. Drain and mix with the aubergines and peppers.

4. Mix the vegetables with the anchovy mixture. Gently stir in the avocado slices.

5. Arrange the radicchio leaves in serving bowls. Spoon in the vegetable and anchovy mixture. Sprinkle with the bacon. Serve with bread.

Preparation time: 15 min
Cooking time: 15 min
Serves 4

3 pickled anchovy fillets, drained
2 tbsp capers
1 red onion, chopped
4 tbsp white wine vinegar
5 tbsp olive oil
2 tsp grated horseradish
salt and pepper, to taste
400g green beans, halved
300g aubergine, sliced
1 red pepper, cut into strips
1 avocado, peeled, pitted and sliced
1 small head radicchio
5 slices cooked bacon, diced

Duck breast with pears, watercress and walnuts

Preparation time: 15 min
Cooking time: 30 min
Serves 4

4 duck breasts
salt and pepper, to taste
100g chopped walnuts
1 tbsp oil
3 pears, thickly sliced
1 tbsp honey
4 tbsp balsamic vinegar
1 bunch watercress

1. Slash the duck breasts with a sharp knife and rub in salt and pepper to taste.

2. Cook in a dry frying pan over a low heat for 6–8 minutes on each side, until cooked through. Pour off the fat and set aside.

3. Add the walnuts to the pan and cook for a few minutes until lightly toasted. Remove and set aside.

4. Add the oil to the pan and cook the pears until just golden. Add the honey and balsamic vinegar to the pan and warm through.

5. Slice the duck breasts and arrange on serving plates with the watercress, walnuts and pears. Drizzle over the honey mixture and serve immediately.

Salad niçoise

1. For the dressing: mix the ingredients together, season with salt and pepper and set aside.

2. Preheat the oven to 400°F (200°C).

3. Bring a large pan of salted water to a boil and cook the potatoes until tender. Drain well and set aside. Cut the potatoes in half if they are large.

4. Rub the tomatoes with a little oil and roast in the oven for 10 minutes.

5. Blanch the beans in boiling water for 5 minutes, drain and refresh in cold water. Pat dry with kitchen paper.

6. While the potatoes are still slightly warm, combine all the ingredients and toss in the dressing. Garnish with mint leaves.

Preparation time: 15 min
Cooking time: 30 min
Serves 4

For the dressing:
2 shallots, very finely chopped
3 tbsp white wine vinegar
1 tbsp grain mustard
7 tbsp olive oil
salt and pepper, to taste

For the salad:
400g new potatoes
200g cherry tomatoes
200g green beans
200g canned tuna, drained of oil
100g pitted black olives
4 canned anchovies, sliced thinly
*   into strips*
1 handful rocket, washed
mint, to garnish

Savoury melon salad in hollowed-out melon

1. Halve the melons and remove the seeds. Hollow out the melons with a spoon, scooping the flesh into a bowl.

2. Mix the melon flesh with the cress and diced pepper.

3. Heat the butter in a frying pan and cook the turkey cubes until golden. Remove and drain on kitchen paper. Set aside to cool.

4. Stir the turkey into the melon mixture and season to taste with salt and pepper.

5. Whisk together the vinegar and olive oil.

6. Spoon the melon mixture into the hollowed-out melon shells. Drizzle with the dressing and garnish with rocket.

Preparation time: 15 min
Cooking time: 15 min
Serves 4

2 Galia melons
1 punnet salad cress
1 large red pepper, diced
1 tbsp butter
300g boneless turkey breast, cut
*   into small cubes*
salt and pepper, to taste
8 tbsp balsamic vinegar
4 tbsp olive oil
rocket, to serve

Preparing
an avocado

Avocado adds a soft, creamy texture to salads, but it must be prepared as close to serving as possible as the flesh turns brown when exposed to the air.

STEP 1 Using a sharp knife, cut all the way around the avocado through to the stone, then carefully pull the two halves away from each other to separate.

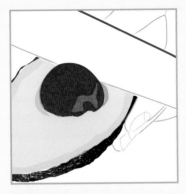

STEP 2 Strike the stone with the knife blade until it embeds. Pull away the knife and the stone should come with it.

STEP 3 Once the stone has been removed, take each avocado half and cut it in half again lengthwise.

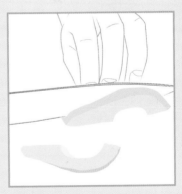

STEP 4 Carefully peel away the skin from each avocado quarter, starting at the top.

STEP 5 Once all the quarters are peeled, slice the avocado lengthwise or cut into chunks.

Fried goats' cheese with dates

1. Coat the goats' cheese in flour, then dip in the egg. Coat in flour again.

2. Heat 2 tablespoons oil in a frying pan and fry the cheese for 2–3 minutes on each side, until golden. Remove and set aside.

3. Heat the remaining oil in the pan and cook the dates until golden.

4. For the dressing: whisk all the ingredients together. Stir in the almonds and peppercorns and season to taste with salt and pepper.

5. Place the cheese and dates on serving plates with the radicchio leaves. Drizzle over the dressing.

Preparation time: 10 min
Cooking time: 10 min
Serves 4

450g goats' cheese, thickly sliced
110g flour
2 eggs, beaten
4 tbsp oil
12 dates, pitted and halved

For the dressing:
3 tbsp cider vinegar
110ml apple juice
50ml olive oil
4 tsp Dijon mustard
1 tbsp honey
1 tbsp chopped almonds, toasted
1 tsp black peppercorns
salt and pepper to taste
radicchio leaves, to serve

Warm salad of broad beans, pancetta and feta with lemon and herb dressing

1. Cook the broad beans in boiling water until just tender, then drain well.

2. Heat the oil in a frying pan and cook the pancetta until crisp and golden. Drain on kitchen paper.

3. Add the garlic to the pan and cook for 2–3 minutes until softened.

4. For the dressing: whisk together all the ingredients and season to taste with salt and pepper.

5. Stir the dressing into the warm beans and add the pancetta and garlic. Season to taste with ground black pepper.

6. Stir in the salad leaves and divide between serving plates. Scatter the cheese over the salad.

Preparation time: 15 min
Cooking time: 15 min
Serves 4

450g broad beans
2 tbsp olive oil
110g pancetta, diced
2 garlic cloves, crushed
2 handfuls mixed salad leaves
200g feta cheese, crumbled

For the dressing:
5 tbsp olive oil
2 tbsp white wine vinegar
1 tbsp Dijon mustard
2 tbsp chopped mixed herbs
salt and pepper, to taste

Apple salad with spinach and cheese

1. Mix the spinach, apples, dates and cheese in a large bowl.

2. Whisk together the walnut oil, vinegar, salt and pepper to taste, until thickened.

3. Toss the dressing with the salad and garnish with fresh herbs.

Preparation time: 15 min
Serves 4

200g baby spinach
4 red apples, cored and sliced into
  matchsticks
8 dried dates, pitted and sliced
175g Cheddar cheese, thinly sliced
100ml walnut oil
50ml cider vinegar
salt and pepper, to taste
fresh herbs, to serve

Chickpea salad with orange and peppers

Preparation time: 15 min
Cooking time: 1 h 30 min
Serves 4

500g dried chickpeas, soaked
overnight
2 red peppers, diced
4 spring onions, sliced
2 oranges, juice
1 orange, segmented
4 tbsp white wine vinegar
2 tbsp lemon juice
6 tbsp olive oil
parsley sprigs, to serve

1. Put the chickpeas into a large pan and cover with water. Bring to a boil and simmer for 1½ hours until tender. Drain and set aside.

2. Mix together the remaining ingredients and stir in the chickpeas.

3. Divide between serving bowls and garnish with parsley.

Chard salad with pine nuts and raisins

1. Whisk together the mustard, vinegar, oil, salt and pepper until thickened.

2. Toss the chard leaves and beansprouts in the dressing and arrange in a serving bowl.

3. Scatter over the pine nuts and raisins.

Preparation time: 15 min
Serves 4

2 tsp Dijon mustard
2 tsp red wine vinegar
2 tbsp extra virgin olive oil
salt and pepper, to taste
4–5 handfuls chard leaves, torn
75g beansprouts
60g pine nuts, toasted
60g raisins

Mixed salad with egg and herbs

1. Boil the eggs for 10 minutes, them immediately cover with cold water. Set aside.

2. Whisk the vinegar and oil until thickened. Season to taste with salt and pepper.

3. Peel the eggs and cut into quarters.

4. Toss the vegetables and eggs gently in the dressing and divide between serving bowls. Garnish with parsley and thyme.

Preparation time: 10 min
Cooking time: 10 min
Serves 4

4 eggs
2 tbsp white wine vinegar
4 tbsp olive oil
200g lettuce leaves
1 handful beansprouts
1 red onion, thinly sliced
salt and pepper, to taste
parsley and thyme sprigs, to serve

Redfish with mint and corn salad

1. Heat the sherry and 5cm water in a frying pan. Add the fish and bring to a simmer. Cook for 3–5 minutes until the fish flakes easily when tested with a fork. Remove the fish and drain on kitchen paper. Chill for about 30 minutes.

2. For the dressing: whisk together all the ingredients and season to taste with salt and pepper.

3. Divide the lettuce leaves between 4 serving bowls. Place the fish on top and scatter over the smoked salmon and mint leaves. Serve with the dressing separately.

Preparation time: 10 min
  plus 30 min chilling
Cooking time: 10 min
Serves 4

4 fish fillets
2 tbsp dry sherry
1 lamb's lettuce

For the dressing:
1 tsp sugar
1 tsp mustard
1 lemon, juice
2 garlic cloves, crushed
5 tbsp olive oil
2 tbsp sherry vinegar
1 tsp cumin seeds, toasted in a
  hot pan
salt and pepper, to taste

To garnish:
110g smoked salmon, finely chopped
mint leaves

Chicory salad with Roquefort, apple and walnuts

Preparation time: 5 min
Serves 4

4 heads chicory, outer leaves
removed and sliced in half
lengthways
1 green apple, cored and sliced
1 stalk celery, sliced
100g Roquefort, crumbled
50g walnut halves
salt and pepper, to taste
6 chives, chopped

1. Arrange the chicory, apple, celery, Roquefort and walnuts on a plate, season with salt and pepper and garnish with the chopped chives.

Warm apple and red cabbage salad

1. Heat the oil in a large frying pan and cook the shallot until soft.

2. Add the honey and cumin and pour in the wine, vinegar, apple juice and lemon juice. Add the cabbage, cover and simmer for 20 minutes, stirring occasionally, until the cabbage is tender.

3. Add the apple slices and cook for a further 5 minutes. Season to taste with salt and pepper. Serve warm.

Preparation time: 10 min
Cooking time: 40 min
Serves 4

2 tbsp oil
1 shallot, diced
1 tsp honey
1 tsp ground cumin
100ml red wine
2 tbsp red wine vinegar
100ml apple juice
½ lemon, juice
½ head red cabbage, cut into strips
2 apples, peeled, cored and sliced
salt and pepper, to taste

Lentil salad with fried pumpkin and goats' cheese

1. Blanch the pumpkin in boiling salted water for about 5 minutes. Drain and pat dry.

2. Heat 2 tablespoons oil in a large pan and gently fry the garlic. Add the pumpkin and cook until tender and starting to brown.

3. Arrange the lentils on plates with the pumpkin, rocket and cheese.

4. Mix together the remaining oil, cider vinegar and balsamic vinegar. Season with salt and pepper and drizzle over the salad.

Preparation time: 15 min
  plus 12 h soaking
Cooking time: 30 min
Serves 4

800g pumpkin, skinned, seeds
  removed and cubed
6 tbsp olive oil
2 garlic cloves, crushed
400g tinned lentils, drained
  and rinsed
1 bunch rocket
150g chopped hard goats' cheese
2 tbsp cider vinegar
1 tsp balsamic vinegar
salt and pepper, to taste

Baked fruit salad

1. Place all the fruits in a bowl. Add the sherry, sugar and orange juice and toss to combine. Cover and stand overnight.

2. Preheat the oven to 350°F (180°C). Butter a baking dish.

3. Put the fruit and liquid into the baking dish. Add the star anise.

4. Cover and cook for 30–40 minutes, until the liquid is bubbling and the fruits are very soft. Remove from the oven and cool slightly.

5. Spoon onto a serving plate and serve warm.

Preparation time: 20 min
plus 12 h soaking
Cooking time: 40 min
Serves 4

375g mixed fruits, e. g. apricots,
apples, peaches, figs, grapes
300ml sherry
1 tbsp light brown sugar
250ml orange juice
3 star anise

Greek salad

1. Mix together all the ingredients, seasoning to taste with salt and pepper.

2. Put into a serving bowl and garnish with parsley.

Preparation time: 10 min
Serves 4

2 onions, sliced
5 tbsp black olives, pitted
200g feta cheese, cubed
4 tomatoes, quartered
½ iceberg lettuce, torn
1 cucumber, peeled and sliced
1 green pepper, sliced
5 tbsp extra virgin olive oil
2–3 tbsp lemon juice
salt and pepper, to taste
parsley sprigs, to serve

Roast pumpkin and Gorgonzola salad

1. Preheat the oven to 400°F (200°C).

2. Cut the pumpkin into slim wedges and cut each in half. Brush with a little of the oil and place on a baking tray. Bake for 20–30 minutes or until tender. Remove from the oven and let cool.

3. Mix the remaining oil with the balsamic vinegar, season with salt and pepper and set aside.

4. Arrange the spinach on serving plates, add the cooked pumpkin and Gorgonzola and drizzle over the balsamic dressing.

Preparation time: 15 min
Cooking time: 30 min
Serves 4

1 medium pumpkin, peeled and
*   seeds removed*
150ml olive oil
2 tbsp balsamic vinegar
200g baby spinach
salt and pepper, to taste
325g Gorgonzola cheese, crumbled

Beetroot salad with apple and chives

Preparation time: 10 min
Serves 4

4 pickled cucumbers, thinly sliced
50ml pickled cucumber liquor
2 red apples, thinly sliced
350–400g cooked beetroot, sliced
2–3 tsp finely grated horseradish
2 tbsp chopped chives
salt and pepper, to taste

1. Toss all the ingredients together in a bowl, seasoning with salt and pepper to taste.

Beef salad with mixed vegetables

1. Heat the oil in a frying pan. Season the meat with salt and pepper and cook for 2 minutes. Remove from the pan and set aside.

2. Deglaze the frying juices with soy sauce and stock and season to taste.

3. Arrange the salad vegetables on serving plates and place the meat on top, while still hot. Drizzle with the sauce and serve immediately.

Preparation time: 15 min
Cooking time: 5 min
Serves 4

1 tbsp oil
400g beef fillet steaks,
*   thickly sliced*
salt and pepper, to taste
4 tbsp soy sauce
4 tbsp beef stock
½ cucumber, sliced into
*   thin ribbons*
100g Swiss chard leaves
100g beetroot leaves
1 carrot, sliced into thin ribbons
1 chilli, very finely chopped
1 red onion, sliced

Warm chorizo and potato salad

1. Cook the potatoes in salted boiling water for 20–30 minutes until tender. Drain and halve.

2. Heat the oil in a pan and fry the potatoes and chorizo until golden brown.

3. Place the radicchio in a bowl and add the potatoes and chorizo. Add a little water to the liquid in the pan and pour over the salad.

4. Stir in the vinegar and the herbs and season with salt and ground black pepper to taste. Serve immediately.

Preparation time: 5 min
Cooking time: 40 min
Serves 4

800g small potatoes
2 tbsp olive oil
400g chorizo sausage, thinly sliced
1 radicchio, torn into bite-sized
  pieces
4 tbsp white wine vinegar
4 tbsp mixed herbs, e.g. chives,
  cress, oregano, basil

Pepper salad with sesame

1. Put the peppers in a pan and cover with water. Bring to a boil and cook for 5–6 minutes, until partially softened. Drain, sprinkle with salt and allow to cool for 20 minutes.

2. Slice the peppers, discarding the seeds and pith.

3. Mix together the garlic, oil and vinegar in a bowl. Season to taste with salt and pepper. Add the sliced peppers, cover and leave to stand for 1 hour.

4. Put the peppers and dressing in a serving bowl and sprinkle the sesame seeds over the top.

Preparation time: 15 min
plus 20 min standing,
1 h marinating
Cooking time: 15 min
Serves 4

2 yellow peppers
2 green peppers
2 garlic cloves, finely chopped
70ml extra virgin olive oil
50ml white wine vinegar
3 tbsp sesame seeds

Asparagus and vegetable salad with fried Norway lobster

Preparation time: 15 min
Cooking time: 20 min
Serves 4

2 x 1 kg cooked lobsters, shells
  removed, cut into serving pieces
1 tbsp ginger wine
1 tbsp cornflour
salt and pepper to taste
oil, for frying
4 courgettes, sliced
12 asparagus spears
parsley, to serve

For the dressing:
1 tsp Dijon mustard
½ tsp salt
½ tsp ground black pepper
2 tbsp lemon juice
2 tbsp white wine vinegar
60ml olive oil

1. Mix together the lobster, ginger wine, cornflour, salt and pepper.

2. Heat the oil in a wok to come 5cm up the sides. Cook the lobster in batches for 2 minutes. Drain on kitchen paper.

3. Cook the courgette slices for a few minutes until softened.

4. Cook the asparagus in a pan of salted boiling water for 5–8 minutes until tender. Drain and rinse in cold water. Drain well.

5. For the dressing: whisk all the ingredients together.

6. Toss the asparagus and courgettes in the dressing.

7. Place the vegetables on serving plates with the lobster. Garnish with parsley.

Red rice salad with red kidney beans, feta and dill

1. Cook the rice according to the pack instructions. Drain and rinse in cold water. Tip into a bowl and toss with the vinegar, oil and seasoning to taste.

2. Add the remaining ingredients and toss again.

3. Divide between serving plates and garnish with dill flowers.

Preparation time: 15 min
Cooking time: 25 min
Serves 4

300g Camargue red rice
2 tbsp red wine vinegar
4 tbsp extra virgin olive oil
100g feta cheese, cut into cubes
2 tbsp pine nuts, toasted
2 red onions, sliced
2 tbsp chopped dill
400g canned kidney beans, drained
dill flowers, to serve

Thai salad with lime, shrimps and peanuts

1. Toast the peanuts in a dry frying pan and set aside.

2. Heat the oil and gently cook the chilli, garlic and ginger for 3–4 minutes until softened.

3. Increase the heat and add the shrimps, then pour in the fish stock and simmer for 4 minutes. Season with salt, pepper and add the chilli powder, soy sauce, oyster sauce and lime juice.

4. Pour boiling water over the glass noodles and leave to stand for 5 minutes. Drain, rinse with boiling water and drain again.

5. Stir the noodles into the shrimp sauce. Garnish with the chopped coriander and toasted peanuts.

Preparation time: 15 min
Cooking time: 20 min
Serves 4

4 tbsp chopped peanuts
4 tbsp oil
1 red chilli, finely chopped
2 garlic cloves, finely chopped
1 piece ginger, 4cm
200g shrimps
150ml fish stock
2 pinches chilli powder
2 tbsp soy sauce
1 tbsp oyster sauce
juice of 1 lime
200g glass noodles
3 tbsp chopped coriander, to serve

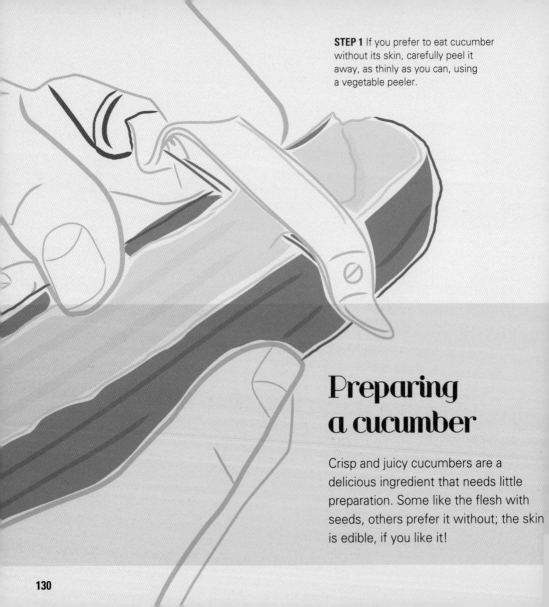

STEP 1 If you prefer to eat cucumber without its skin, carefully peel it away, as thinly as you can, using a vegetable peeler.

Preparing a cucumber

Crisp and juicy cucumbers are a delicious ingredient that needs little preparation. Some like the flesh with seeds, others prefer it without; the skin is edible, if you like it!

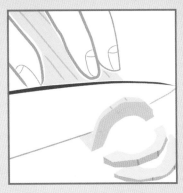

STEP 2 Cut the cucumber in half lengthways and place the halves seed-side up on a chopping board. Scoop out the seeds using a teaspoon.

STEP 3 Turn over each scooped-out cucumber half, so that the curved side is uppermost, then cut into chunky slices using a sharp knife.

STEP 4 For a decorative effect, score the cucumber skin. This is best done with a channel knife, but if you don't have one, use the prongs of a fork.

STEP 5 Leaving the cucumber whole, and using a very sharp knife, cut along the length of the cucumber to make very thin slices.

Artichoke and orange salad with rosemary

1. Sprinkle the artichokes with lemon juice to prevent them turning brown.

2. Heat the oil in a pan and cook the artichokes and garlic for a few minutes until softened. Season to taste with salt and pepper and pour in the water.

3. Add the rosemary to the pan, cover and bring to a boil. Simmer gently for 15 minutes. Drain and leave to cool.

4. Peel the oranges, removing the white pith and divide into segments, over a bowl to catch the juice.

5. Put the juice in a pan with the butter and honey and bring to a boil. Simmer for 2 minutes.

6. Pour the orange juice mixture over the artichokes and stir in the orange segments.

7. Put into a serving bowl and garnish with rosemary and thyme.

Preparation time: 20 min
Cooking time: 20 min
Serves 4

12–16 baby artichokes
2 lemons, juice
4 tbsp olive oil
2 garlic cloves, crushed
salt and pepper, to taste
150ml water
4 sprigs rosemary
4 oranges
2 tbsp butter
1 tbsp honey
rosemary and thyme sprigs, to serve

French bean salad with shallots and pine nuts

1. Cook the beans in plenty of boiling salted water for about 8 minutes, until al dente.

2. Heat the oil and butter in a pan and fry the shallots over a medium heat. Add the pine nuts and toast quickly. Add the sugar and cook until slightly caramelised.

3. Stir in the vinegar. Drain the beans and add to the pan. Stir well and season to taste with salt and ground black pepper. Serve warm or cold.

Preparation time: 15 min
Cooking time: 15 min
Serves 4

600g French beans
2 tbsp oil
2 tbsp butter
250g shallots, quartered
100g pine nuts
1 tsp sugar
6 tbsp white wine vinegar

Warm beef salad with carrots and tamarind

1. Preheat the oven to 400°F (200°C). Heat the oil in a roasting tin and brown the meat on all sides. Cook for 10–20 minutes, depending on how rare you like your meat. Remove from the oven, wrap in foil and leave to rest in the turned-off oven.

2. Arrange the vegetables on serving plates. Slice the beef and put on the plates.

3. For the dressing: whisk together all the ingredients until the sugar has dissolved. Drizzle the dressing over the salad.

Preparation time: 15 min
Cooking time: 20 min
Serves 4

1 tbsp oil
500g piece beef sirloin
175g beansprouts
110g cherry tomatoes, halved
2 shallots, finely chopped
4 carrots, sliced into ribbons

For the dressing:
2 tbsp tamarind paste
2 tbsp fish sauce
2 tbsp soy sauce
1 lime, juice
2 tbsp palm sugar

Potato salad with chives and mustard

Preparation time: 5 min
Cooking time: 35 min
Serves 4

1kg small, waxy potatoes
200g mayonnaise or soured cream
 (or more, depending on taste)
salt and pepper ,to taste
1 large red onion, sliced
½ bunch chives, snipped
3–4 tbsp wholegrain mustard

1. Cook the potatoes in boiling salted water for about 20 minutes, until tender. Drain well.

2. Mix the warm potatoes with the mayonnaise or soured cream and season with salt and pepper.

3. Divide between serving bowls and scatter with onion and chives. Add small dabs of mustard and leave to cool.

Fish salad in a smoked salmon basket

1. Mix all the ingredients together, except for the smoked salmon and melba toast. Season to taste with salt and pepper.

2. Divide the mixture among the salmon slices, placing it onto the middle of each slice. Fold the salmon around the filling to make a neat parcel.

3. Serve with melba toast.

Preparation time: 5 min
Cooking time: 10 min
Serves 4

1 smoked trout fillet, flaked
110g soft cream cheese
juice of 1 lemon
10 chives, snipped
1 tsp horseradish sauce
1 tbsp double cream
4 slices smoked salmon, each about
   13cm square
salt and pepper, to taste
melba toast, to serve

Green pasta salad

1. Cook the spaghetti according to the pack instructions.

2. Heat the butter and oil in a frying pan and cook the leek, celery and pepper until soft. Remove from the pan and drain on kitchen paper.

3. Cook the mangetout in boiling water for about 5 minutes until tender.

4. Drain the spaghetti and mix with the vegetables, stock, vinegar and celery leaves. Season to taste with salt and pepper and leave to stand for 10 minutes.

5. Transfer to a serving bowl and garnish with basil. Serve warm or cold.

Preparation time: 15 min
   plus 10 min standing
Cooking time: 20 min
Serves 4

250g spaghetti
2 tbsp butter
2 tbsp oil
1 leek, sliced
1 stick celery, sliced
1 red pepper, diced
200g mangetout
50ml vegetable stock
6 tbsp white wine vinegar
2 tbsp chopped celery leaves
salt and pepper, to taste
basil leaves, to serve

Shrimp salad

1. Whisk together the oil, vinegar and lemon juice and season to taste with salt and pepper.

2. Mix with the shrimps, crab and vegetables and season with salt and cayenne pepper.

3. Divide between 4 serving bowls and garnish with coriander.

Preparation time: 10 min
Serves 4

4 tbsp sunflower oil
3 tbsp white wine vinegar
1 tbsp lemon juice
salt and pepper, to taste
300g cooked shrimps
300g cooked crab meat
2 tomatoes, skinned and quartered
2 red peppers, diced
2 shallots, diced
150g celery, thinly sliced
cayenne pepper
1 tbsp chopped coriander, to serve

Autumn salad with baked pumpkin

Preparation time: 15 min
Cooking time: 55 min
Serves 4

1 pumpkin, cut into thick slices
olive oil
salt and pepper, to taste
2 red onions, cut into wedges
1 bulb fennel, quartered
1 tbsp capers
4 tbsp extra virgin olive oil
2 tbsp fresh lemon juice
chicory and mint leaves, to serve

1. Preheat the oven to 400°F (200°C).

2. Put the pumpkin slices into a roasting tin and season with salt and pepper. Drizzle with oil and cook for 30 minutes.

3. Add the onions and fennel to the roasting tin and drizzle with oil. Cook for a further 20–25 minutes, until the vegetables are tender. Remove from the tin and leave to cool.

4. Stir together the capers, extra virgin oil and lemon juice. Season to taste with salt and pepper. Pour over the vegetables and toss gently.

5. Put onto serving plates and garnish with chicory and mint leaves.

Sautéed strawberries and cherries with pine nuts

1. Toast the pine nuts in a dry frying pan until lightly browned. Set aside to cool.

2. Melt the butter in the frying pan. Add the sugar and vanilla pod and stir until the sugar has dissolved.

3. Add the cherries and strawberries to the pan and cook for 3–5 minutes, stirring occasionally, until the fruits are tender and heated through. Add a squeeze of lemon juice, stir, then remove from the heat. Stir in the cinnamon, if using.

4. Remove the fruit with a slotted spoon and place on a serving plate. Sprinkle with the pine nuts.

5. Add the wine to the juices in the pan and bring to a boil. Cook until the liquid is reduced and syrupy. Allow to cool and pour over the fruit. Decorate with the vanilla pod and strawberry leaves.

Preparation time: 15 min
Cooking time: 20 min
Serves 4

75g pine nuts
4 tbsp unsalted butter
4 tbsp light brown sugar
1 vanilla pod
900g yellow and red cherries, pitted
450g strawberries
juice of 1 lemon
1 tsp ground cinnamon (optional)
200ml red wine
strawberry leaves, to serve

Lentil and onion salad with fresh herbs

1. Put the lentils in a pan with 1 sliced onion and the bouquet garni. Cover with water and bring to a boil. Cover and simmer for 25 minutes. Leave to stand for 5 minutes, until the water is almost completely absorbed.

2. Remove the bouquet garni and tip the lentils into a bowl.

3. Whisk together the vinegar and olive oil. Stir in the herbs and season to taste with salt and pepper.

4. Add half the dressing to the warm lentils and onions and mix well.

5. Divide between serving dishes and drizzle over the remaining dressing.

6. Heat the butter in a frying pan and cook the onions until soft and just golden. Drain and place on top of the lentil salad.

Preparation time: 15 min
Cooking time: 35 min
Serves 4

225g Puy lentils
2 onions, sliced
1 bouquet garni
2 tbsp balsamic vinegar
6 tbsp extra virgin olive oil
2 tbsp chopped mixed herbs
salt and pepper, to taste
1 tbsp butter

Penne with prawns and peas

1. Cook the penne according to the instructions on the packet.

2. Heat the butter in a frying pan and cook the prawns for a few minutes until cooked through. Remove and set aside.

3. Add the garlic to the pan and cook for 3 minutes. Stir in the peas and cream and bring to a boil. Season to taste with salt and pepper.

4. Mix the cornflour with a little water and stir into the pan until thickened. Add the prawns to the pan.

5. Drain the pasta and mix with the contents of the pan and season with salt and pepper.

6. Divide between 4 serving bowls and garnish with the dill.

Preparation time: 10 min
Cooking time: 20 min
Serves 4

300g penne
2 tbsp butter
300g prawns
1 garlic clove, finely chopped
100–150g peas
200ml double cream
salt and pepper, to taste
1 tbsp cornflour
2 sprigs dill, to serve

Asian egg noodle salad with chicken and vegetables

1. Heat 2 tablespoons sesame oil in a frying pan and cook the chicken and squid for a few minutes until cooked through. Set aside to cool.

2. Cook the green beans in a pan of boiling salted water for 5 minutes. Drain and cool.

3. Heat the remaining oil in the pan and cook the peppers and onion until soft. Drain and set aside to cool.

4. Cook the noodles according to the instructions on the pack. Drain and mix with the soy sauce, fish sauce and hoisin sauce.

5. Toss all the ingredients together and season to taste with salt and pepper. Serve warm or cold.

Preparation time: 10 min
Cooking time: 15 min
Serves 4

3 tbsp sesame oil
200g chicken breast, thickly sliced
200g squid, cut into rings
1 handful green beans
1–2 red peppers, cut into strips
1 onion, sliced
½ small Chinese cabbage, shredded
1 handful young spinach
250g egg noodles
2 tbsp light soy sauce
1 tbsp fish sauce
1 tbsp hoisin sauce
salt and pepper, to taste

Spinach and avocado salad, with bacon

1. Divide the spinach, avocados and onion between 4 plates and season with salt and pepper.

2. Fry the bacon in a dry frying pan until crisp and brown. Add the walnuts to the pan and toast until lightly browned.

3. Spoon off most of the bacon fat from the pan, reduce the heat and add the olive oil until warmed through.

4. Remove from the heat, add the vinegar and mustard and whisk until thickened.

5. Chop the bacon and scatter over the salad with the walnuts. Drizzle with the warm dressing.

Preparation time: 15 min
Cooking time: 10 min
Serves 4

200g young spinach
2 avocados, sliced
1 small onion, thinly sliced
salt and pepper, to taste
10 rashers lean bacon
100g chopped walnuts
3–4 tbsp olive oil
2 tbsp white wine vinegar
3 tsp Dijon mustard

Raw tuna with basil on glass noodles

Preparation time: 20 min
  plus 1 h marinating
Cooking time: 5 min
Serves 4

4 lemons, juice and zest
2 garlic cloves, crushed
1 onion, diced
4 tbsp olive oil
450g very fresh tuna loin, thinly
  sliced
salt and pepper, to taste
250g glass noodles
juice of 2 limes
1 tbsp finely grated ginger
3 tbsp shredded mint leaves
2–3 tbsp beansprouts
1 tbsp sweetcorn
basil leaves, to serve

1. Mix together the lemon juice, zest, garlic, onion and oil with the tuna slices. Season with salt and pepper. Cover and chill for 1 hour.

2. Pour boiling water over the noodles and leave to soak for 5 minutes.

3. Whisk together the lime juice, ginger and mint.

4. Drain the noodles and toss with the dressing. Set aside for 10 minutes to allow the flavours to infuse. Add the beansprouts and sweetcorn and mix until well combined.

5. Divide between 4 serving bowls and place the marinated tuna on top. Garnish with basil.

Apple and celery salad with rice

1. Core the apples and slice thinly, tossing them immediately in the lemon juice in a large bowl. Add the celery and rice.

2. Whisk the cream until thick, then fold in the yoghurt and apple juice. Pour over the apple mixture, and toss gently to coat.

3. Divide between serving bowls and serve immediately, garnished with snipped chives.

Preparation time: 20 min
Serves 4

4 green eating apples
1 tbsp lemon juice
2 sticks celery, sliced
250g cooked rice
50ml double cream
200ml plain yoghurt
3 tbsp apple juice
snipped chives, to serve

Thai squid and pork salad

1. Heat the oil and gently cook the garlic and chillies until softened.

2. Pour in the rice wine and stock, then stir in the honey, ginger and soy sauce. Add the pork and squid to the pan, then cover and cook gently over a very low heat for 5 minutes.

3. Transfer to a bowl and mix with the shallots, vinegar and sesame oil. Season to taste with salt and pepper.

4. Divide between serving bowls and sprinkle with mint and coriander.

Preparation time: 20 min
Cooking time: 10 min
Serves 4

1 tbsp oil
2 garlic cloves, crushed
2 chillies, finely chopped
4 tbsp rice wine
200ml chicken stock
1 tsp honey
1 tsp finely grated ginger
2 tbsp light soy sauce
400g pork fillet, cut into thin strips
400g squid, cut into thin strips
2 shallots, sliced
2 tbsp rice vinegar
1 tbsp sesame oil
salt and pepper, to taste
1 tbsp each chopped mint and
    coriander, to serve

Thai salad with chicken and mint leaves

1. Put the curry paste ingredients into a mortar and grind to a paste.

2. Mix the chicken with the curry paste and lemongrass.

3. Heat the oil in a wok or frying pan and brown the chicken on all sides then stir-fry for 2 minutes. Remove the chicken and set aside.

4. Add the onion to the wok and cook for 2 minutes, then add the tomatoes and chicken and cook gently for 5 minutes.

5. Arrange the herb and salad leaves and spring onions on serving plates and place the chicken, tomatoes and onion on top.

6. Heat the sugar, fish sauce and lime juice in the wok. Drizzle over the salad and garnish with lemongrass, coriander and mint.

Preparation time: 20 min
Cooking time: 15 min
Serves 4

For the curry paste:
2 chillies
1 shallot
½ tsp ginger, freshly grated
1 tsp shrimp paste

For the salad:
450g boneless, skinless chicken, cut into strips
1 tsp lemongrass, finely grated
1 tbsp oil
1 onion, chopped
2 tomatoes, cut into wedges
1 handful mint leaves
1 handful coriander leaves
400g mixed salad leaves
1 bunch spring onions, sliced
1 tbsp brown sugar
2 tbsp fish sauce
2 tbsp lime juice

To garnish:
lemongrass, finely shredded lengthways
coriander and mint leaves

Potato salad with smoked trout

Preparation time: 20 min
Cooking time: 20 min
Serves 4

800g new potatoes
4 tbsp soured cream
2 tbsp mayonnaise
2 tbsp white wine vinegar
salt and pepper, to taste
1 red onion, sliced
2 spring onions, sliced
400g smoked trout, flaked
2 tbsp capers
1 punnet salad cress
2 tbsp parsley, chopped

1. Wash the potatoes and boil for about 20 minutes or until tender. Drain, let cool a little then peel and roughly chop.

2. Mix the soured cream, mayonnaise and vinegar and season with salt and pepper.

3. Mix with the dressing with the potatoes, onion and spring onions and spoon onto plates.

4. Put the trout on top of the salad, scatter with capers and herbs and serve.

Grilled pears with Stilton

1. Heat the grill.

2. Cut the pears in half and remove the cores. Brush the pear flesh with lemon juice.

3. Grill the pears for 2–3 minutes on each side until browned. Remove and set aside.

4. Place the watercress on serving plates and arrange the pears on top.

5. Crumble over the cheese and sprinkle with walnuts.

6. For the dressing: mix all the ingredients together in a bowl and season to taste with salt and pepper.

7. Drizzle the dressing over the salad and serve immediately.

Preparation time: 15 min
Cooking time: 6 min
Serves 4

4 firm pears
2–3 tbsp lemon juice
300g watercress
225g Stilton cheese
75g chopped walnuts

For the dressing:
3 tbsp walnut oil
3 tbsp olive oil
1 tsp mustard
2 tbsp white wine vinegar
1 pinch sugar
1 tsp peppercorns, lightly crushed
salt and pepper, to taste

Caesar salad with chicken

1. For the croutons: rub the bread with the garlic. Heat half the oil in a frying pan and fry until crisp and golden. Drain on kitchen paper.

2. Heat the remaining oil and fry the chicken until golden and cooked through. Set aside to cool.

3. For the dressing: whisk all the ingredients together until thick. Season to taste with salt and pepper.

4. For the salad: arrange the lettuce leaves in serving bowls. Scatter over the croutons and chicken.

5. Drizzle over the dressing and garnish with grated Parmesan cheese.

Preparation time: 20 min
Cooking time: 15 min
Serves 4

For the croutons:
3 thick bread slices
2 garlic cloves, crushed
4 tbsp oil

For the dressing:
1 garlic clove, crushed
1 tsp lemon juice
½ tsp English mustard
1 tsp Worcestershire sauce
2 egg yolks
100ml olive oil
pinch sugar
2 tbsp grated Parmesan cheese
 plus 3 tbsp to serve
1–2 anchovy fillets
salt and pepper, to taste

For the salad:
4 boneless chicken breasts, thickly
 sliced
1 cos lettuce

Segmenting an orange

Some recipes will call for oranges to be cut into segements and the chewy, less digestible membrane to be removed. This takes a little practice, but is worth the effort.

STEP 1 With a sharp knife, remove a slice from the top and bottom of the orange so you can sit it on a chopping board.

STEP 2 Hold the orange firmly with one hand and with the other work round it, slicing away the peel and pith.

STEP 3 Trim away any remaining pith then cut into the orange, slicing between the segments.

STEP 4 Cut along the edge of the segment, then cut along the other membrane edge to free the chunk.

STEP 5 Repeat with all the segments, then squeeze the leftover membrane into a bowl to catch any juices.

Beef noodle salad

1. Put the noodles in a large bowl and pour boiling water over. Leave until soft, then drain and rinse well with cold water.

2. Heat a frying pan until very hot. Brush the steak with oil and season with salt and pepper. Cook for 1–2 minutes. Remove from the pan and set aside.

3. Heat the butter in the pan. Drain the mushrooms and add to the pan. Cook for a few minutes until golden. Drain on kitchen paper and set aside.

4. For the dressing: whisk together all the ingredients.

5. Toss the drained noodles, steak and vegetables with the dressing. Place on serving plates and scatter with peanuts.

Preparation time: 15 min
Cooking time: 10 min
Serves 4

250g medium rice noodles
600g sirloin steak, thinly sliced
1 tbsp oil
salt and pepper, to taste
1 tbsp butter
40g dried Chinese mushrooms,
*   soaked in warm water for*
*   30 minutes*
½ Chinese cabbage, shredded
3 carrots, cut into thin strips
100g chopped unsalted peanuts

For the dressing:
6 tbsp Thai sweet chilli sauce
juice of 2 limes
2 tbsp fish sauce

Mexican bean salad

1. Heat the oil in a frying pan and cook the onions and garlic until softened. Add the chilli and tomatoes and cook for 2 minutes.

2. Tip into a bowl and stir in the sweetcorn, beans, parsley, vinegar and oil. Season to taste with salt and pepper.

3. Divide between serving plates and garnish with cherry tomatoes.

Preparation time: 10 min
Cooking time: 10 min
Serves 4

1 tbsp oil
2 onions, diced
1 garlic clove, crushed
1 chilli, finely chopped
6 tomatoes, diced
450g canned sweetcorn, drained
450g canned kidney beans, drained
1 tbsp chopped parsley
2 tbsp sherry vinegar
3 tbsp olive oil
salt and pepper, to taste
cherry tomatoes, to garnish

Aubergine salad with mushrooms, pine nuts and mascarpone

1. Preheat the oven to 425°F (220°C).

2. Put the aubergines into a baking dish and drizzle with 3 tablespoons oil. Cook for 25 minutes, then add the mushrooms, remaining oil, a sprinkling of salt and pepper and the garlic. Cook for a further 20–25 minutes until softened and browned.

3. Place the aubergines and mushrooms on serving plates. Scatter with the pine nuts.

4. Place a spoonful of mascarpone on top and garnish with pea shoots.

Preparation time: 15 min
Cooking time: 50 min
Serves 4

2 large aubergines, quartered
5 tbsp olive oil
110g button mushrooms
2 garlic cloves, crushed
salt and pepper, to taste
100g pine nuts
225g mascarpone
pea shoots, to serve

Jersey potato salad with radishes, feta cheese and mint

Preparation time: 15 min
Cooking time: 20 min
Serves 4

350g Jersey Royal potatoes,
  halved
1 red onion, sliced
75g feta cheese, crumbled
5–6 radishes, sliced
1 tbsp chopped oregano
1 tbsp peppercorns, crushed
mint leaves, to serve

For the dressing:
4 tbsp olive oil
1 tbsp red wine vinegar
1 tbsp capers, chopped
1 garlic clove, crushed

1. Cook the potatoes in salted boiling water for 15–20 minutes until tender. Drain well and leave to cool.

2. Gently mix the potatoes with the salad ingredients in a large bowl.

3. For the dressing: whisk all the ingredients until well blended. Pour over the salad and toss thoroughly.

4. Put the salad on a serving plate and garnish with mint.

Tomato and mozzarella tower

1. Heat the oil in frying pan and add the tomatoes and cook for 1 minute on each side. Remove and set aside.

2. Cook the mozzarella slices for 1 minute on each side.

3. Layer the tomato and mozzarella slices to form 4 'towers'.

4. Place on serving plates.

5. Whisk the basil, vinegar, peppercorns and oil and drizzle over the 'towers'. Garnish with rocket.

Preparation time: 10 min
Cooking time: 5 min
Serves 4

1 tbsp olive oil
4 large firm tomatoes, cut into
*   20 slices*
450g mozzarella cheese, cut into
*   20 slices*
6 large basil leaves, torn
1 tbsp balsamic vinegar
2 tsp black peppercorns, crushed
1 tbsp extra virgin olive oil
rocket leaves, to serve

Cobb salad

1. Mix together the salad leaves and place in a salad bowl.

2. Arrange the bacon, avocados, chicken, tomatoes, egg yolks, and whites and cheese over the leaves. Sprinkle with the chives.

3. For the dressing: whisk together the ingredients and serve with the salad.

Preparation time: 15 min
Serves 4

1 head Romaine lettuce, shredded
1 head frisée, shredded
½ bunch of watercress, torn
6 slices cooked bacon, diced
2 ripe avocados, pitted, peeled and
    chopped
350g cooked chicken breast, diced
2 tomatoes, chopped
2 hard-boiled eggs, separated, the
    yolk finely chopped and the white
    finely chopped
50g grated cheese
2 tbsp snipped chives

For the dressing:
70ml red wine vinegar
1 tbsp Dijon mustard
1 tsp sugar
130ml extra virgin olive oil

Orzo with vegetables and feta

1. Cook the pasta in plenty of salted water according to the pack instructions.

2. Cook the shallots in the oil, add the peppers and asparagus and continue frying for a few minutes.

3. Stir in the tomato paste and vegetable stock and simmer for about 4 minutes until the vegetables are cooked but still firm and the liquid has almost completely evaporated.

4. Stir in the lemon zest, basil and drained pasta and toss well. Season to taste with lemon juice, salt and pepper.

5. To serve, crumble the feta over the pasta, scatter with pine nuts, arrange on plates and garnish with salad leaves.

Preparation time: 20 min
Cooking time: 20 min
Serves 4

400 orzo
*2 shallots, peeled and finely
  chopped*
3 tbsp olive oil
2 red peppers, roughly chopped
2 yellow peppers, roughly chopped
*500g Thai asparagus, chopped
  diagonally into 3cm pieces*
1 tsp tomato paste
100ml vegetable stock
zest and juice of ½ lemon
1 tbsp freshly chopped basil
salt and pepper, to taste
100g feta cheese
*2 tbsp chopped pine nuts, toasted in
  a skillet without oil*
lettuce leaves, to serve

Grilled fruit salad

Preparation time: 10 min
Cooking time: 10 min
Serves 4

1kg mixed fruits, e.g. apples,
  grapes, pineapple, plums
3 tbsp lemon juice
2 tbsp light brown sugar

To decorate:
2 tbsp icing sugar
mint leaves
raspberries

1. Heat the grill. Grease the grill pan.

2. Halve and stone fruits such as plums and apricots; cut large fruit such as pineapple, into wedges.

3. Toss in the lemon juice and brown sugar.

4. Grill the fruit for about 3 minutes on each side, until lightly browned. Allow to cool.

5. Arrange the fruit on serving plates and sift over the icing sugar. Decorate with mint leaves and raspberries.

Feta cheese and pomegranate salad

1. Put the cheese in a serving bowl, pour over the lemon juice and oil and scatter over the garlic. Leave to marinate for 3 hours.

2. Place the beetroot leaves on top of the cheese.

3. Scatter over some pomegranate seeds and place the parsley and mint on top. Sprinkle with the remaining pomegranate seeds.

Preparation time: 10 min
   plus 3 h marinating
Serves 4

350g feta cheese, cubed
juice of 1 lemon
2 tbsp extra-virgin olive oil
2 garlic cloves, crushed
1 handful beetroot leaves, cut into
   strips
1 pomegranate, seeds removed
1 handful parlsey leaves
1 handful mint leaves

Greek tortellini salad

1. Heat 2 tablespoons olive oil in a frying pan and cook the peppers and courgettes for about 4 minutes until tender. Remove from the pan and drain on kitchen paper.

2. Mix the remaining oil with the lemon juice and zest, herbs and salt and pepper to taste. Mix with the peppers and courgettes.

3. Cook the tortellini according to the pack instructions and drain well.

4. Mix together the tortellini, vegetables, cheese and olives. Season to taste and divide between serving bowls.

Preparation time: 15 min
Cooking time: 25 min
Serves 4

6 tbsp olive oil
2 small red peppers, diced
2 courgettes, chopped
juice and finely grated zest of
  1 lemon
1 tsp thyme leaves
1 tsp chopped rosemary leaves
1 tbsp chopped parsley
salt and pepper ,to taste
200g tortellini
200g feta cheese, crumbled
125ml black olives, pitted and sliced

Preparing melon balls and slices

Beneath their tough, textured skin, melons have a sweet flesh; they are best eaten chilled and chopped up as close to serving as possible for maximum juiciness.

STEP 2 Hold each half with one hand and scoop out the seeds in the middle using a spoon. Discard these.

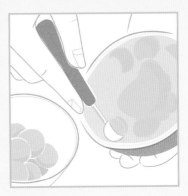

STEP 3 Using a melon baller, scoop out balls of flesh all around the melon half, avoiding the edges of the skin.

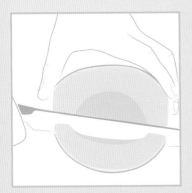

STEP 4 If you prefer to serve slices, hold the melon half in one hand and cut into slices.

STEP 5 Once sliced into small pieces, take a sharp knife with a flexible blade and cut the melon flesh from the skin.

Insalata del contadino

1. Preheat the oven to 400°F (200°C). Grease a baking tray.

2. Place the sliced vegetables on the baking tray and sprinkle with salt and pepper and 1 tablespoon oil. Cook for 20 minutes. Remove from the oven and drizzle with 2 tablespoons oil and the lemon juice and leave to stand for at least 1 hour.

3. Sprinkle half the balsamic vinegar over the vegetables. Layer the courgettes, squash and peppers, toasted bread and cheese. Top with a basil leaf and an aubergine slice.

4. Drizzle the remaining balsamic vinegar over the top.

Preparation time: 20 min
  plus 1 h standing
Cooking time: 20 min
Serves 4

1 courgette, sliced
salt and pepper, to taste
1 small yellow squash, sliced
2 red peppers, sliced
1 aubergine, sliced
3 tbsp olive oil
2 tbsp lemon juice
4 tbsp balsamic vinegar
8 rounds toasted bread
4 slices Scamorza cheese
4 large basil leaves

Fish and mango salad

1. Season the fish with salt and pepper and lightly dust with flour.

2. Melt the butter in a frying pan. Place the fillets in the pan, floured side down. Fry gently for 4–5 minutes, then turn the fish in the pan and remove from the heat. Leave to stand for a further 2–3 minutes, then remove from the pan and set aside to cool.

3. Place the remaining ingredients in a bowl and toss together, seasoning to taste with salt and black pepper.

4. Put the salad into serving bowls. Cut or flake the fish into pieces and arrange on top of the salad. Garnish with lime slices.

Preparation time: 20 min
Cooking time: 5 min
Serves 4

4 × 175g firm white fish fillets, skinned
salt and pepper, to taste
flour
1 tbsp butter
1 red pepper, diced
juice of 2 limes
2 small mangoes, peeled and sliced
2 spring onions, finely chopped
8–10 lettuce leaves, torn
1 tbsp chopped coriander leaves
4 tbsp olive oil
black pepper
lime slices, to garnish

Tuna and pasta salad

1. Heat the oil in a frying pan and cook the mushrooms until tender and golden. Stir in the peas and cook for 2 minutes.

2. Cook the pasta according to the packet instructions and drain.

3. Toss the warm pasta with all the other ingredients and divide between 4 serving bowls.

Preparation time: 10 min
Cooking time: 20 min
Serves 4

2 tbsp olive oil
150g mushrooms, sliced
150g peas
150g pasta tubes
150g canned tuna, drained
150g canned sweetcorn, drained

Bean salad with red mullet

Preparation time: 15 min
Cooking time: 20 min
Serves 4

1 tbsp butter
8 small red mullet fillets
400g broad beans
2–3 red peppers, skinned and cut
　into wedges
1 handful Brussel sprout leaves
4 tbsp olive oil
1 small onion, diced
1 garlic clove, finely chopped
1 tomato, diced
1 tbsp chopped thyme
4 tbsp vegetable stock
4 tbsp white wine vinegar
2 tsp pink peppercorns, crushed
sea salt

1. Heat the butter and gently fry the red mullet fillets over a low heat for 3 minutes.

2. Cook the beans in a pan of boiling, salted water for 5–8 minutes.

3. Blanch the peppers in boiling, salted water for 2 minutes. Add the Brussel sprout leaves for the last minute. Drain the Brussel sprout leaves, peppers and beans, rinse in cold water and drain well.

4. Heat 1 tablespoon oil and cook the onion, garlic and tomato gently until soft. Add the thyme, stock, remaining oil and the vinegar.

5. Remove from the heat and add the peppercorns.

6. Reserve half of the dressing and carefully mix the rest with the fish and vegetables.

7. Arrange on serving plates and garnish with the remaining dressing. Sprinkle with sea salt and serve.

Carrot and tuna salad

1. Mix together the carrots and tuna.

2. Whisk together the oil, vinegar, lemon juice, mustard and peppercorns, until thickened.

3. Divide the carrot and tuna salad between 4 serving plates and drizzle with the dressing.

4. Garnish with lemon wedges and coriander.

Preparation time: 15 min
Serves 4

8 carrots, coarsely grated
150g canned tuna, drained
  and flaked
6-8 tbsp olive oil
4 tbsp wine vinegar
3 tbsp lemon juice
2 tbsp Dijon mustard
2 tsp green peppercorns
lemon wedges and coriander,
  to serve

Green lentil and SunBlush tomato salad with spicy lamb skewers

1. Mix the honey, olive oil, ras el hanout and thyme together and smear over the lamb. Place the lamb in the fridge and allow to marinade for 1 hour.

2. Cook the red rice according to the pack instructions. Drain the rice and mix with the lentils, sunblush tomatoes and chopped parsley.

3. Thread the lamb cubes onto the skewers and grill for 15 minutes under a hot grill, turning the skewers halfway through cooking.

4. Whisk together the dressing ingredients and stir into the lentil mixture. Add in the rocket and combine. Top the salad with the lamb skewers and serve.

Preparation time: 1 h
Cooking time: 25 min
Serves 4

3 tbsp honey
2 tbsp olive oil
8 tsp Ras el hanout
1 tsp chopped fresh thyme
400g lamb leg steak, cut into small
    cubes
200g can Puy lentils
200g red rice
100g sunblush tomatoes
3 tbsp chopped flatleaf parsley
40g rocket leaves
4 bamboo or metal meat skewers

For the dressing:
juice of 1 lemon
60ml walnut oil

Pumpkin and orecchiette pasta salad with sage pesto

1. Cook the pasta in a large pan of salted boiling water according to the pack instructions. Steam the pumpkin cubes for 15 minutes or until easily pierced with the tip of a knife.

2. Using a mini food processor, blend the pesto ingredients until smooth.

3. Mix the pasta with the pumpkin and pesto. Toss in the rocket and serve.

Preparation time: 10 min
Cooking time: 20 min
Serves 4

200g orecchiette pasta
220g pumpkin, cut into cubes
25g rocket leaves

For the pesto dressing:
100ml extra virgin olive oil
25g sage leaves
30g walnuts
30g grated Parmesan

Piccalilli salad with English mustard dressing

Preparation time: 10 min
Cooking time: 5 min
Serves 4

250g fine green beans
3 carrots, peeled
3 asparagus spears
3 baby cauliflower heads
2 small red onions, cut into rings
15 radishes, finely sliced
20 chives, cut in half
40g mixed leaves

For the dressing:
60ml rapeseed oil
30ml cider vinegar
2 tsp English mustard
1 tbsp Greek yoghurt
1 finely chopped cornichons
1 tbsp finely chopped tarragon

1. Blanch the beans for 3–4 mins before plunging them into cold water and draining. Shave the peeled carrots and asparagus spears into a large salad bowl. Break the cauliflower in to small florets and add to the bowl along with the remaining salad ingredients.

2. To make the dressing, whisk together the oil and vinegar before adding in the mustard, yoghurt, cornichons and tarragon. Season to taste.

3. Pour the dressing over the salad ingredients and toss. Serve with leftover cold meats such as beef or lamb.

Pancetta and spinach salad with toasted macadamia nuts

1. Under a hot grill, cook the pancetta until crispy and cut each slice into 3 horizontally.

2. To make the dressing, cut the tomato into quarters, remove the seeds and grate the fleshy part, leaving the skin behind into a small bowl. Whisk in the rest of the dressing ingredients.

3. Place the spinach in a salad bowl and crumble in the blue cheese. Add in the macadamias and crispy pancetta.

4. Dress the salad by pouring over the dressing and tossing the leaves to coat them.

Preparation time: 5 min
Cooking time: 10 min
Serves 4

10 slices of pancetta
120g baby spinach leaves
100g Gorgonzola cheese
80g toasted macadamia nuts

For the dressing:
1 tomato
60ml extra virgin olive oil
30ml cider vinegar
1 tsp Dijon mustard
1 tbsp crème fraîche
1 tbsp chopped parsley

Quinoa superfood salad

1. Put the pumpkin cubes into a baking tray and toss in a little olive oil, the cinnamon and sugar. Place in a preheated oven and roast for 20–25 minutes or until soft and browning round the edges.

2. Cook the quinoa and giant couscous separately according to the packet instructions. Blanch the asparagus in hot water for 2–3 minutes. When the pumpkin, asparagus and grains are cooked, combine with the sprouted lentils, seeds, avocado, pomegranate and chopped herbs.

3. Squeeze the remaining pomegranate seeds over a large bowl, removing the juice and discarding the leftover seed. Whisk together with the remaining dressing ingredients with the pomegranate juice. Pour over the salad, toss and serve.

Preparation time: 10 min
Cooking time: 25 min
Serves 4

120g pumpkin, cut into cubes
olive oil
¼ tsp cinnamon
1 tsp sugar
150g quinoa
50g giant couscous
12 fine asparagus spears, blanched
30g sprouted lentils
1 tbsp pumpkin seeds
1 tbsp sunflower seeds
1 ripe avocado, peeled and
   roughly diced
½ pomegranate, deseeded
1 small bunch of mint, finely
   chopped
1 small bunch of flatleaf parsley,
   finely chopped

For the dressing:
juice of 1 lemon
50ml extra virgin olive oil
10ml pumpkin seed oil
seeds from ¼ of a pomegranate
1 tsp pomegranate molasses .

Index

Notes

Notes

Notes

Notes

Notes

Favourite recipes

Favourite recipes

Favourite recipes

Favourite recipes

Favourite recipes